OBITS.

tess liem

Coach House Books, Toronto

first edition

Published with the generous assistance of the Canada Council for the Arts and the Ontario Arts Council. Coach House Books also acknowledges the support of the Government of Canada through the Canada Book Fund and the Government of Ontario through the Ontario Book Publishing Tax Credit.

LIBRARY AND ARCHIVES CANADA CATALOGUING IN PUBLICATION

Liem, Tess, 1985-, author
    Obits / Tess Liem.

Poems.
Issued in print and electronic formats.
ISBN 978 1 55245 376 6 (softcover).

    I. Title.

PS8623.I363O25 2018   C811'.6   C2018-903924-8
                                      C2018-903925-6

Obits. is available as an ebook: ISBN 978 1 77056 573 9 (EPUB);
ISBN 978 1 77056 574 6 (PDF)

Purchase of the print version of this book entitles you to a free digital copy. To claim your ebook of this title, please email sales@chbooks.com with proof of purchase. (Coach House Books reserves the right to terminate the free digital download offer at any time.)

This book is for my extended family

There is no innovating loss. It was never invented, it happened as something physical, something physically experienced. It is not something an 'I' discusses socially.
– Claudia Rankine

For years I have been hiding behind that: being addicted to fatalism can make one look calm, capable, even happy.
– Yiyun Li

Table of Contents

III. Rewrites

IV. Yesterday, in future tense

I. Theories

It sinks
like a stone, this attention to the lives
of others.
– Wendy Xu

Dead theories

1

At sixteen, I tried
to dye my hair blonde. You could say
this was my mistake.

Blonde,
a colour between golden & light chestnut.
Blonde
with an exceptional -e
distinguishing genders.

I've never seen a light chestnut
& my hair turned orange & crispy.

Now I fantasize
about meeting blondes.
Like

Laura Palmer,
Dora Lange,
Alison DiLaurentis,
Lilly Kane

casually on my commute,
but they ask me
to wait for the next train.

Ruth Stone wrote
My hazard wouldn't be yours, not ever,

But every doom, like a hazelnut, comes down
To its own worm.

& I tuck her name into my memory,
a compassionate hard pain,
a hazelnut in my shoe.

Hazelnut
another shade of blonde.

2

After the screens above the metro platform reported
forty-nine dead in Orlando,
someone told me
a man with platinum hair
& his own TV show
broke down crying reading their names.
What did that do.

I write names of missing & murdered women
in a notebook.
I set up alerts.
I add up.
Each day a new sum.
What does that do
is the same as asking
What doesn't that do.

I doubt they want to be poems.

Hair colour is not noted in a statistic.

Maybe
if blonde & thin with straight teeth,
those dead are less anonymous.
Maybe
(impossible) to theorize the real.

One morning a journalist says
Imagine if there was any kind of balance
whatsoever where we knew the names
of any of the victims of the indiscriminate
violence of [our] government[s].

I know Laura, Dora, Alison, Lilly.

They probably dyed their hair. But it worked
didn't it? They're dead, but fake dead, &
it's easier to be fake dead than fake alive, isn't it?

3

In *Clueless* one thing Cher & D. do to Tai
is dye her hair. They knew better than to try blonde
& I knew better than to try again. I went dark
red or purple. Colours others only notice
under very bright light
or if I were lying in the snow.

Hitchcock said
Blondes make the best victims…

like a virgin snow that shows up
the bloody footprints.

4

I wouldn't pit myself against a blonde.
My best friend in high school was a natural.
All the boys who had crushes on her
would make out with me at parties
then offer to give her a ride home.

Well, fair enough.

All we all wanted was her sandy attention.

5

So.

I know the names of some dead blondes on TV.

So what, I think about dying daily.

I don't have a dead girl theory.

I don't need dead girl modelled for me.

6

Drop a scarf.

If you are blonde,
studies show someone
will pick it up for you.
If you are not alone.
If you work hard enough & you are likable.
If you are not discouraged too easily
& you exercise & get enough fibre.
If you can accept love.

7

Hannah Gamble,
a blonde poet I like, wrote
I have to admit, sometimes
I want nothing more than to be lying on the bottom
of an unimpressive river.

& I have to admit
you don't have to be
the ice cold,
the bombshell,
the light chestnut.
You don't have to
wander around in snow
to feel numb.

You don't have to
close your eyes
& hold your breath
to fake dead.

8

I don't mind being lost
in the snow,
feeling dumb,
but I leave a trail of chestnuts
just in case
footprints aren't enough.

9

Snow,
because winter forces me to imagine flaxen weather.
Even though
when I look forward to spring
it feels like a risk.

When

I may appear melancholic

When the object of my mourning is   missing

When no obit.   is printed

When a body   an addend to a sum   a number on a screen

When no one agrees on the numbers

When you encourage forgiveness & gloss over resentment

When an identity   a trope

When mourning is not accessible
where accessible means legible
where legible means understood
where understood means validated
where validated means proved
where proved means facts
where facts don't offend

When you think healing comes from emphasizing resilience
rather than destruction

When some lives count & others are counted

When you believe *the disturbance of self-regard is absent*
in mourning

When mourning is not sanctioned

When it was not nothing   lost

When grief is not granted it is never-ending

& I may appear melancholic

The jilt

So really & no surprise

Freud doesn't specifically mention women
in 'Mourning and Melancholia'

Kind of like how, historically, mostly male mice
are used for medical testing

Except one appears, she pops in parenthetically
(e.g., a betrothed girl who has been jilted)

Because *melancholia, too, may be the reaction
to the loss of a loved object.*

So say *The jilted ex is merely melancholic* five times fast

Every day for your whole life in some way say it

Say *Snap out of it*

Or why not read into it

Jilt used to be a noun; *jillet*, a flirtatious girl

We lost that meaning

Just kidding, not really

I'm pretty sure it wasn't lost on Freud

So say the ex is the jilt & the jilted

& say there is no etymology so perfect as to hear *jail* in *jilt*

No jailed jilters

Say *Who cares about those melancholy flirts anyway*

Really, though, who is caring for them?

Call it

In some moment of conceptual energy

I attempt an inventory

49   6   14

                    9   1,000+

A wish to be meticulous

Having failed, I call the numbers a poem

Does a body rise or fall into a statistic?

Unearthed, we say, & never *earthed* instead of *buried*

The ground never not uneven

The distribution of corporeal vulnerability
is a non-poetic phrase I repeat

I repeat it is uneven

Step over the potholed thing

Call the step a poem

& this poem a longing
& this poem a lengthening
& this poem a lung

See how pointing is a poem

(Fondly, a demonstrative monster)

How lovely and how doomed this connection of everyone with lungs
is a phrase I must have misunderstood

Call the air we all breathe a poem

Call me a wish to be mellifluous

Having misstepped, I'm bitter

I wanted a poem to be a throat clearing

My misunderstanding

There is a point at which you must jump into the hole
in order to keep digging

To speak as if we all share the same loveliness, the same doom,
is not to speak

of the fact that some people have their hands
around other's necks

Aesthetic distance

This time, though, I'm having a hard time moving on,

As a witness to my distance

because I don't just see the images as documents of atrocity,

I write a lyric of witness

I also see them as aesthetic;

Which is a lyric of distance

& that doesn't sit easily

Which is a lyric of uneasiness

with the other way of seeing them.

Which is a lyric of specific focus

Indeed it feels immoral.

& if you're barely paying attention you know

It feels wrong.

So Lyric of self-hate, help me dissolve my complicity

I'm having a hard time moving on

Away from a persistent depression

Lyric, you know, some days that's all there is

& look how the poet – how I circle back on myself
   continually

What to make of this sadness!

What does it do!

Obit.

An obsolete. & what to do with
bits of news, brief footage on screens

subtitled, underground, on our commute.
Obits. add up, like, say, seventy-four

some summer day. That number
revised, rises. Obit., an arithmetic.

We get on the train, shoulder to shoulder,
we go downtown. I count

how many people are
too close to me.

Show us the bodies.
Tell us their names.

I love you obits. when you
disappear you're easier to miss.

~~Obit.~~
Memorial

....
....
....
....
....
....
....
....
....
....
....
....
....
....
....
....
....
....
....
....
....
....
....
....
....
....
....
....
....
....
....
....
....

~~Obit.~~
~~Memorial~~
Proof

Empedocles took a leap into Mount Etna
to prove he was a god
& no one has seen him since.

~~Obit.~~
~~Memorial~~
~~Proof~~
Story

Euripides wrote about how Hecuba
turned into a dog because her grief
for her two children, at the end of the Trojan War,
was too much to keep her human.

~~Obit.~~
~~Memorial~~
~~Proof~~
~~Story~~
News

[…] went missing
to prove nothing
& no one has seen them since.

~~Obit.~~
~~Memorial~~
~~Proof~~
~~Story~~
~~News~~
~~Poem~~
Theory

Break the soil
& burrow into an omitted obit.

One written & not published
is a non-notice,
is anon.

Take yourself underground
to wait for the same train daily.

An obit., a non-fiction, is a story
we have to tell ourselves.

Did you know you can subscribe to news
from Obitsarchive.com?

Some obits. without effort.
Unfold your grief.

I've given the obits. too much credit.

Another dead theory:
An obit. unpublished is an instance
of something buried to keep it safe.

An obit. delayed becomes a memorial,
if it becomes. It becomes a makeup
for the loss of a loss.

Ride the train from end to end all day, exit
where you entered & stretch your stiff limbs.
Make your grief public.

Imagine if I knew the names
of all the people, everyone
waiting for this train.

~~Obit.~~
~~Memorial~~
~~Proof~~
~~Story~~
~~News~~
~~Poem~~
~~Theory~~
Data

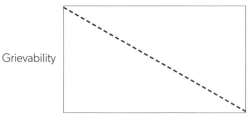

Grievability

Vulnerability

The data suggests
the more vulnerable you are,

the less likely
anyone who didn't already know you

will know you after.
Just kidding.

There is no data.
The fear of grief

& the impulse to manage it
have a particular direction.

It is a fear of certain grief,
a fear of a collection of certain data.

Imagine if everyone waiting for
the same train knew your name.

~~Obit.~~
~~Memorial~~
~~Proof~~
~~Story~~
~~News~~
~~Poem~~
~~Theory~~
~~Data~~
Finding

I wait on the metro platform

Where people gather daily

Underground without ceremony

Where I am tired, hungry, & still

Where I find my interest in elegy

Is exceeded by my interest in death.

II. Ibu, saudara, isteri

what nationality
or what kindred and relation
what blood relation
– Theresa Hak Kyung Cha

Opo tumon, hayo?*

opo: yes or what

An email.
A bold new number in my inbox.
My father.
My last aunt on my father's side.
Maybe pancreatic cancer (?).
Late August.
Late Aunt.
No one would agree or say what exactly.
Yes it was morning here so what.
It was night in Indonesia.
What to make of the difference.
I still don't know.

tumon (ton): to be mistaken (about what one has seen); to (be able to) see; to observe; to have seen; to see, watch, witness

Aunt Hoei mostly in pictures.
Her hair a tide of black curls.
Her hands clasped together.
Her glasses slightly tinted.
Her clothing soft, smooth, & bright.
A picture of a picture of her on flowers
    surrounded by flowers surrounded.

* *Opo tumon, hayo* is a Javanese saying to express amazed disbelief. The approximate translation is 'have you ever seen such a thing?'

hayo: (usage: exclamation) for shooing away animals, etc.

My father booked a trip to Indonesia that ended up being too late, so in his email to us he wrote, 'I was hoping to see her but…' His ellipsis shooing away what he didn't want to say. & Aunt Hoei, Thian Hoei, steps in & out of my memory again, again, my grief, a timid animal.

Of course we have doubt

Which family by blood & which by law.

We are a language you didn't learn.

I felt related to Uncle Chung Jean even if I didn't tell.

When we feel haunted, it is the pull of our old home we're experiencing, but a more upsetting possibility is that the past has become homeless.
Yiyun Li, 2017

His dark grey hair, & wide quiet smile assured me. We were a we.

We are a history you research.

If it weren't the truth, I wouldn't believe there were ever any mangoes bought, sold, or eaten in Hometown, Alberta.

Maybe no we grew up there.

At the kitchen table my father cut the sweet & sour fruit

we ate slice by slice.

Form by form, Uncle Chung Jean taught me tai chi. The art of shifting weight around your body slowly & what I barely remember, I've learned since, is wrong.

We are not so much disappearing as much as we are a distance.

The mango in one hand, knife in the other, a slick, shrinking yellow sculpture.

We who try to verify our memories often find facts don't help:

Was it in '92 or '93? The World Series we watched sitting on a picnic blanket in our living room.

Sometimes we are like birds thudding into windows.

Watch video clips of Joe Carter's home run.

We won!

That was '93. On a blue & white gingham blanket, we got macaroni salad on the carpet.

Look how we all pile on to each other.

Maybe it was the same year in Jogja when someone tall enough picked a mango from the tree next to the driveway & shared it with me. Maybe not.

What is it in me would
devour the world to utter it?
Li-Young Lee in 1990

Uncle Chung Jean pushing energy away, inviting it back.

We are a fruit that doesn't need to be washed
if the dirt is clean & tended to. You don't need
to put the red-green skin in your mouth,
but why wouldn't you.

Once, a lover called me yellow on the way to a baseball game.

A cut through our we.

That one sours, closer to the seed.

This crowd has hollered itself weak.
Vin Scully in '93.

Uncle Chung Jean died a few years before his wife, Aunt Djan,
did. Djan looked like my father like my brothers look like him
like I look like them

so *aunt* is like *sister once removed* – why don't we put it
that way?

Which by blood & which by law &

what nationality
or what kindred and relation
what blood relation
Theresa Hak Kyung Cha in '82.

Some kinship words haunt me.

'Opa' and 'Oma' may be more familiar to Indonesians.
It is widely used across Indonesia, particularly by the Chinese.
Tenissa in 2018.

Some language by blood & some by law,
& some takes root where it is planted.

& what common knowledge I have of Aunt Hoei. Thian Hoei
of Temanggung. Her hometown central, an area on a map, high-
lighted pink. I find facts like silkworms, honey, & soy oil. I keep
looking.

I remember that father wrote our genealogy
in a book with Chinese characters.
Unfortunately, none of us could read it,
and we don't know what happened to that important book.
I suspect it is now lost!
Uncle Seit in 2015.

This knowledge repeats!

This crowd has hollered itself weak.

Wheat, barely, canola, & beef. What kind of *we* grew up around
me. Hometown told my mother, & she told me, it was impressed
how she kept our mixed-race family together.

We were a question if not questioned

& I expect to be corrected – to be told there are better ways to
cut a mango than the slow peel toward the seed, but I'm done.
I've scraped the yellow flesh off the skin with my teeth.

Obit.

A habit. Every time
you see the train doors open

slow your pace because
death feels like a crowd

you could wedge yourself into
if you ran toward it, but you won't

because you don't mind waiting
underground at some stations

where there is no cellphone signal,
no way to tell anyone anything

without speaking
how would you know if she were still alive

if you saw her again
you might not run toward her

because every time you try to write her elegy
you're stuck with the facts of an obit.

What anyone might know.
This failure a repeat.

Your mourning, an archipelago
with too many islands to name or know.

Ibu, saudara, isteri

Aunt Hwie (like *we*)
was, I learned, Aunt Hoei (like *oui*)
was Bibi Hoei to me
& The Thian Hoei (like *thé, tiens, oui*)

Father, in English, took Joseph,
is Sioe An (like *Sue Ann*),
is Bapak to me,

& we spelled
her name wrong repeatedly.

Uncle, in English, took Joseph, too,
is Sioe Siet (like *sue seat*),
is Paman to me,

& he didn't correct us all along
until now & Hoei,
in English, took Josephine.

As it goes
ibu, saudara, isteri,

are as unknown to me as *Hoei,*
are *mother, sister, wife,*

& Hoei was *oui* was *we*
was

Obit.

A distance   & I am allowed
        long   lapses of remembering

Days without thinking   loss
She is a place I am allowed to visit

I am allowed distance   I am a loud distance
        Bodies too close together are loud too

Two people spooning next to the busker
between the escalator   & the platform this morning

Most days we are together like a riddle
What stands still while it moves?

I'm tired of being touched
by everyone   I'm tired of death

On the metro   we keep to ourselves
I read strangers' texts

A conversation consisting of only
red heart emojis

Fold our arms against our ribs
We haven't a physical distance between us

I don't tell any rush hour
about the fourteen-hour flight

I wasn't asked to take to mourn
my last distant aunt

I don't have to tell
anyone   anything

Thian Hoei from Temanggung

Talk bright to a body
you never knew.

Thian Hoei
like *oui* like *yes* like *we.*

Temanggung, a sound
you have not heard.

Ask an honest question.

How do you know
yourself when

you don't know
your family?

Speak of an heirloom
as if you were holding it.

How do you unearth
what was never buried?

Obit.

A secret. Once she called you yellow,
       no lie, at a yellow light on the way
              to a baseball game & you let her
                     run across the street

without you. A swing
       & a miss. You wanted to walk home
              to punish yourself for not
                    standing up for yourself
                  but didn't.

You haven't enjoyed baseball since '93
       but you wanted to go because
              the tickets were free & you like crowds
                    & expected to get to yell.

Walking down Spadina Avenue
       through Chinatown, after eating dumplings
              without mention of ancestry

or how Aunt Hoei told you
       you'd be a model movie star in Indonesia,
              & how you knew but didn't say,

she was talking about your mixed
                  race
                face.

It feels like a lie when
        someone from your extended family –
                someone you barely knew – just died.
                & if not yellow,

your lover would have found something else
        you barely knew about yourself
                to call out. At dusk in the stadium

when the big lights clunk on
        & the grass-stained pitcher
                walks the batter to first base

the crowd is quiet &
        grief, like a swing,
                hits you out of the park.

Exact fraction

1/2

She is off-white, right? Off-white, exactly right. Not exactly
white. Which white exactly? Which fraction white? She is
visibly off-white. She is a visible frac-
tion. Her visibility though minor is divisible,
right? Rather, her minor visibility isn't visi-
ble enough exactly. She is white-washed,
right? She is exactly half-white, right?
Half-white exactly. An exact fraction.
She has privilege, right? Her
privilege is off-white. Not
exactly right. She is not
not privileged. Not
exactly. Not an
exact fraction.

Each fraction takes space. Each fraction takes too much
space. She takes place in too many spaces. She is
half. She is an exact fraction. An excellent
fraction. Each half exactly half. Exactly.
She numerates, she denominates,
she divides, she
fractures
exactly.

But she says she is not half.
Rather, she is two.

She has two voices:
one sounds like this

the other sounds like *this*
(or sometimes like (this)).

The tone of each voice
is nearly identical in pitch

so when they speak in unison
& they always do, the difference –

the slight difference in frequency
generates a beat.

Two voices
meaning only

to maintain her pulse,
the vibration of her heart,

& language is a consequence.
She is the hum in the room.

Even in sleep
she must murmur:

A hummingbird's heart can beat
260 times a minute

to support the whipping
of its wings. But she thinks

the wings beat the heart.
Her two voices cinch

both halves: the chamber
that pushes, the chamber that pulls.

The slight difference in frequency generates a beat

I spent some night or day watching a video over & over. It was not the one of a dog hugging another dog or the one of frogs gathering to watch a video of worms, or the one of a goat head-butting a mirror. When I looked for this video again, no configuration of search terms would surface it. It was taken down or under 220,000 other results.

& I surprised myself with feeling at the loss of such a nothing thing.

This video featured a person at a lab bench, framed from shoulders to waist, in a white coat. They stood behind two tuning forks attached to wooden boxes & this person did not speak. One mallet tap & both vibrate. The tone soothed me while subtitles explained. The un-struck tuning fork resonated in sympathy with its twin.

A weight is then attached to one & both are struck & *the slight difference in frequency generates a beat.*

A sentence like this is a skipping stone: when found it is admired briefly before it's flicked into the water, made to do a trick.

So some day or night, this video over & over. It was like Aristophanes' story about twins, too. How once we had four arms & four legs. Over & over because I was not interested in leaving bed with so few limbs. Over & over because I was wondering whether I ought or ought not write myself into halves. Over & over I broke myself into lines. I made an inside joke with myself where one half fixed a weight to the other, & I let the beat fascinate.

My last name's last name

I thought it would be easy,
easy to talk about trees.

Tree is a word that refers to a thing,
a thing or an idea of a thing, a thought.

A thought expressed out loud, if understood,
is understood as language. Try, two trees.

Two trees in English means two trees.
Two tree characters in a row, in Chinese,

Chinese people have told me,
mean forest, but you'd say lim in Chinese. Three trees,

tree characters, I mean,
might mean big forest, so who says
language is arbitrary?

An arbitrary 'e' was added by the Dutch.
When the Dutch added themselves to Indonesia,

Indonesia forget how to say Lim.
Lim became Liem, or that's what I'm told.

Told by people who are not my father.
My father doesn't even specify one syllable or two.

Two trees, two syllables,
two things, too many things I don't know I mean.

Obit.

An exception.

When one February day felt like August,
rain was a sound

she returned & the *click click click*
of the radiator expanding & contracting –

it was not like a lung.
The smell of dust burning

was not like an answer.
I mean, I remembered her

& it was exceptional.
An obit., an opportunity:

a tumour took over her pancreas.
Opo tumon, hayo?

I never saw the thing.
Instead a philodendron lying flat

on a balcony across the street
& I assumed it was living.

Try to remember this
is a part of a series of failures.

The plant on its side
not something you can just pick up

& how its leaves underwent
winter, green & glossy,

was not like nothing.
I will not turn her into a plant.

I will not unearth her
like that.

Stop looking into the dirt, asking
did grief knock me over

or did it not pick me up.

Inheritance

My own oral tradition began in the kitchen,
(*caught in*)
never learned how to spell *bakwan/batwan*,
(*but when*)
a corn, carrot, onion fritter,
(*a flitter*)
that my father deep-fried in a wok,
(*walk*)
seasoned before I was even a thought.

The kitchen, a linguistic exercise:
sambal, a red chili
olek, a paste
or
sambal, heat &
olek, to grind, or crush
or
sambal, a symbol
& olek: oh, look

& if we never named
anything we ate
what would we have eaten.

Satay, batwan/bakwan, gato gato/gado gado, sambal olek
Father, look, a skewer of flitter salad & a grinding heat

& if we never named
anything we ate
I wouldn't have a language to look for.

My unknowing crushed into a paste,
kept in the fridge,
& inheritance: a wok.

III. Rewrites

What I thought was the body humming reside, reside,
was the body sighing revise, revise.
– Li-Young Lee

My body in three movements (one)

I read we can understand Shakespeare's use
of the word *nothing* as a reference
to zero where zero means a vulva,
at least in his sonnets. I thought how nice:
one of my body parts, in being nothing,
is something. This something enough to know
I want to drop Shakespeare, stop writing, & learn
how to do something useful with my hands.

I thought it out, decided to become
an electrician, & my friend told me
I would make beautiful light art: neon
sculptures shaped like no thing in particular.
Or, my body all wired, lit & bending.
But, no, it's not my thing to move nothing.

My body in three movements (two)

I'll start a queer construction company
to advocate for our rights & I won't
wish for much else. A lie. I'll try reading
again, I'll try writing in the evenings
when I am tired from wiring light.
& I'll try not to romanticize this
literal electricity. But I'll
probably fail. Because, well, honestly,

I am trying to figure out a way
to want to be in the world. & you know
I expect to be told not to put words
like *honestly* in my poems, not to
start with that shit. So I won't start with it.
I won't end with it honestly either.

My body in three movements (three)

I've thought about it & the nothing is
not my body. It is not my body:
a tight fourteen lines. It cannot be mine.
& it would not be my body drunk with
neon lights either. It's easier if
I understand it is not my body
in particular. Easier if I
accept accepted criticism, if
I admit nothing ever happened to
any part of my body, if I lie,
if I have nothing to lose. Easy if
I'm an absence named nothing.
                              I write
o to describe grief & to me it means
I had more than a pen to begin with.

My body in three movements (coda, note to self)

You are not here to clean the dirty
mirror. Do you remember
your body? It is a storm you wait for, leave
every door & window open.
Your politics refer to an attempt to make
some part of yourself safe. Where are you
when your phone signal drops? Don't worry,
one day you will get to go into an electronics store
& trust somebody. Even if all you were ever taught
is to love men & math, even if
the Ragnar Kjartansson exhibit
only moved you literally from room to room,

it's OK. Here:
feel the space between your body & your shadow.

Mother, wife, sister

I have been rewriting stories.
One I read called 'Brothers' goes like this:

A man who works in a bicycle factory in Chicago,
a man who is lonely & in love with a girl,
this man kills his wife & he doesn't know why.

In the framing scenes,
men on a rural roadside in a fog
talk about that man who killed his wife
& those men, they are also lonely
& they also don't know why.

In my rewrite, a woman, a wife,
she is left at home most of the time
& she is barely spoken to
& she doesn't speak
& she is killed
& no reason is given.

I am also lonely
& don't know why.

Mother, wife, sister

What is left after one does a word search for *wife* & deletes every sentence that does not include her:

... (p 1)

[Trained to see ourselves as objects]

A man there has murdered his wife and there seems no reason for the deed (p 2).

[& to be positioned as the Other]

His wife in particular was like some strange unlovely growth that had attached itself to his body (p 3).

[estranged to ourselves]

... (p 4)

One evening, some six weeks ago, the man who worked as a foreman in the bicycle factory killed his wife and he is now in the courts being tried for murder (p 5).

[we have a story]

'Well – there had been a struggle and in the darkness his wife had been killed' (p 6).

[that by definition cannot be self-present to us]

He spoke of the man who has killed his wife and whose name is being shouted in the pages of the city newspaper that come to our village each morning (p 7).

[a story that, in other words, is not a story]

It may be that the dog like the workman's wife and her unborn child is now dead (p 8).

[but must become a story.]

Mother, wife, sister

What unlovely grammar failed you

Into which body did your spirit enter

When his body struggled about & yours fell

What space you took up

Mother, wife, sister

I know your story,

a strange unlovely growth

attached to my body.

& Dear Sherwood, I know

you could not have known that less than 100 years later

some not-wife would take your story,

all 3,569 words,

the wrong way.

I know my reading

is not supported by the text.

It's not that I am not lonely.

I get that.

It's just that you made
the wife

the loneliness.

Obit.

A fossil. Dark yellow, brownish, translucent stone.

I wear an amber ring for superstitious, private reasons.

What do you wear to keep you well?

Rebecca Solnit wrote

*There is a canonical body of literature in which women's
stories are taken away from them*

zeroed, so to speak.

& I'm ashamed to admit I used to love,

without question, *Lolita, light of my life… my sin,*

my soul. I am used,

in other words, to loving what keeps me ill.

You cannot learn about amber without learning about ambergris.

Its sweet wet sandy smell was used as plague repellent.

Grey, waxy, & dull. What Melville called

the essence found in the inglorious bowels of a sick whale.

In other words, a hardened piece of whale vomit in your
pocket will keep you well.

Some Smart Man told Solnit

You don't seem to understand the basic truth of art.

Another tried to convince me I couldn't tell a stone
from dark yellow, translucent plastic.

After Baudelaire

I. Slut, a dialogue
after 'Tu mettrais l'univers entier dans ta ruelle'

You would fuck the whole universe,
you slut.

You, a callus, too boring to be cruel.
Man eater.

A heartless rack,
you're pretty in an ugly way.

Your power & your law of beauty:
a machine, blind & deaf & rich.

A clamp, a cut, a thirst.
Why are you not full of shame?

No mirror reflects
your pain.

You are an expert in hiding.
You are ooze on the tree, not-amber.

Harden into your time,
you beast, you bitch, you sin.

There is a genius of body,
a might in your unknowing,

a light in your awfulness.

II. Swagger
after 'Le Serpent qui danse'

Skin like silk, empty eyes, stinky hair,
you remind me of an ocean

& I'd love to sail around in you; or rather
I'd literally love if you were a boat.

Because seeing you walk around
like you don't care about me,

it actually reminds me of snakes,
lazy ones, baby ones;

or rather, you're more like elephants,
lazy ones, young ones.

& it's amazing how elephants, too,
when they walk, they sway.

They are like water, or a ship;
or rather, they are like a stream

swollen by the thaw, &
when the water of your mouth rises

to the edge of your teeth
it's the surface tension that enthralls me,

that threat of flood – you & your swagger –
that dulls the edge of my art.

III. Yours is mine
after 'Je t'adore à l'égal de la voûte nocturne'

I like you how I like my nights:
sad, quiet, & retreating.

It's adorable, how you shut up & run.
Makes me feel like

I could pluck
the most faraway star from the sky.

Makes me feel like I could climb you
the way maggots swarm a compost bin

& call you a hot mess
then admire what I've done.

Your resistance
a cool blue ornament

I hold. My night,
a vault that holds you.

IV. The generation of a woman

after 'Avec ses vêtements ondoyants et nacrés'

A woman is both
symbolic & strange
like a snake,
like a desert,
like sea foam bearded on a beach,

but I see into her eyes.
For even in being a symbol
she still has a body,
whether it dropped from heaven
or emerged from myth,
she could still wear a string of pearls.

& she doesn't end with me
even if her sterility glitters
like gold,
like steel,
like cubic zirconia.

The woman as symbol
will still breathe & birth
whole cultures of snakes

who write a woman walking in a dress
to be exotic but controlled
by some man with a stick.

Anonymous woman elegy

The story is about the woman
who comes into a cafe three times a week.

It is about how she is a woman
but she is not given a name.

It is about how she died.
About not knowing the woman's name

until she died.
About gathering with strangers to mourn.

It is about the morning the woman died.
The story is about how the woman smiled.

Her teeth.
It is about whether she had a lover,

whether she was loved,
whether she deserved love.

Then suddenly the story is about how the narrator feels bad
about the time she told her mother she hated her.

About whether the narrator deserves love.
For a moment, about the woman.

For another, about everyone. But mainly
the story is about the narrator:

how she can make anything
about anyone

about herself seem like
it's about everyone for a moment.

Adaptation

Am I supposed to believe –

when I see this poster
advertising the adaptation of *Anna Karenina*
from the platform of the metro
every morning, every evening
with Anna's ballerina body bent
like the stem of a leaf
falling or rising
a pose meant
to convey her existential tumult
while a small toy train circles her feet
her fate so diminished
that even if you haven't indulged
in the 700-page tome
even if you never thought to do such a thing
or spent a winter considering your own personal adaptation
her ending is before you
every morning, every evening
on the platform of the metro
& you might think –

Anna was bigger than the train?

Obit.

A body, a testimony,
a story told in code.

Obit., a body, the one they lost in a blackout.
Neon light bent into the shape of a girl.

Obit., a body, a river to follow, or
a feminist theory popularized in the 1980s.

Obit., a body, an omission,
a whisper.

Obit., a body,
an art that can harm.

Elegy for hers

Her heels: mountain peaks.
She sleeps on her stomach,

one arm under the pillow
under her head, finally still

after working all night
the dawn passes without song,

only her yawn. Hers, yes. In sleep

she clings to his rambled demands
& his weather. Yes, his.

& her bones, they hold enough
or too much. Her attention feathers.

Pine & fir: the roughest clouds:
hers.

Quiet, giddy.

I can't say I wanted that

There is more than one way to leave a body
& I've left many behind already. There in the
unceremonious second year of mastering in
The Department of English
I sit at the back of a classroom to which I am assigned
& a professor, who I'm assigned to assist,
he draws a triangle on the blackboard.
This is Literature.
Some students copy. He's dead serious,
he only reads dead men seriously. He put
Katherine Mansfield on the syllabus, but
his sympathy is with her husband who
had to deal with her bisexuality. I can't say

I wanted to write this. Plus
I forgot to note whether Milton or Shakespeare
was the pinnacle. This professor
who has tenure, this professor, who,
in the year two-thousand-seventeen,
was still worried about Lady Gaga's influence –

I can't say I wanted to write
about him & how his life
couldn't pass the Bechdel test.
I can't say I wanted that.

I want praise, not grief.
I want this poem to be an affirmation.

You can laugh at that. I know I need
that kind of relief.

But if I try too hard,
laughter escapes me. I laugh when
I'm nervous. I laugh when some
sadness needs to be shaken out of me.
Like when Marcela told me
there were no writers of colour,
no black writers, no Indigenous writers
in her high school curriculum. Haha.
Same. You can laugh at that. How
I've filled my bookshelves with
stories from which I'm absent. How
my mother is white & my Chinese
co-workers called me white-washed
because I look Chinese but don't speak it.
I laughed at that because, indeed,
my mother bathed me.

But at the back of the classroom
I am neither a good student nor teacher
even when I am serious,
but today I thought
I don't want power, I want capability

which might mean I want a law degree
or I want to learn more about electricity
or I just want to write better poems
because a living writer said
The opposite of love is not hate, it is power

& I believe it
& I pick love, but I want
to be capable of loving.

IV. Yesterday, in future tense

Believe me I am not being modest when I
admit my life doesn't bear repeating.
– C. D. Wright

Obit.

A repeat: *The disturbance of self-regard*
is absent in mourning.

Wrong! One evening my grief is glitter in the escalator
& for a moment, I am euphoric,

distracted by light
caught in steel treads because

I am away from myself for as long as it takes
to get down to the metro platform

where all the people are waiting,
where we gather every day

as if it is no big deal to be together,
where I only look up to look at a screen

at the time of the next train & news about some other place
where the air is bad with obits.

that will not be written up.
Wrong again, I return to myself,

so I guess I have to stop
telling people I am in mourning.

The stoics

Epictetus, born into enslavement, was a stoic
so he would have summed up his circumstance like this:
It could've been worse.

On a good day get out of bed,
go as far as the porch, & stand still.

Stoic as in *stoikos* as in *stoa*, a shelter,
or the place where Zeno of Citium taught.
Stoa may be *sta-* as in to stand,
set down, make, or be firm.

William B. Irving of Dayton, Ohio, a living stoic in 2015, argued
to live stoically meant one would always say
the glass is half full because delight in its fullness
is heightened by the possibility of emptiness.

Stoic sounds close to *stone*, too,
but I feel like a pebble, supposed to take pleasure
in not being totally weathered.

Zeno, Epictetus, & Bill sit in rocking chairs
on my porch because they enjoy the way wood creaks.

Their glasses are empty. I offer them nothing.
They delight in the existence of glass,
how nice to see through it.

You could be a sad stoic
but you would have weapons

you could use to overcome sadness,
says Bill, not thinking of any weapons made of metal.

I put elastic bands around my wrist & snap them.

The stoic would delight – Bill insists on the word
delight, as in a higher pleasure – in a sunny day
precisely because it is not cloudy nor is it raining.

The stoic might wish to be a farmer if he weren't
so high on being a stoic.

Every evening when a parent puts his child to bed,
Bill explained, he should allow for the thought
of his child dying to flicker.

Loss also a problem belonging to the future,
so why not entertain the thought?

The next morning the child is still alive,
but if the stoic did not allow for that flicker,
less delight in his child's life.

Sta- as in status as in protected by statutes.
As in stand, set down, make, or be firm
if nothing holds you down already.

I tell Bill antidepressants don't work for me
& I always let the thought of my own death hover.
If I wake up tomorrow I doubt I'll be filled
with deep & interesting delight.

Bill says he doesn't want to talk to me anymore
if I am always going to be so negative. Bill says
stoicism doesn't prevent grief, but a stoic
will engage in preventative measures.

When a glass is empty it means a thunderstorm
could have been a tsunami. It means control yourself.
It means stay in bed if you feel too weak
to manage your melancholia & don't talk to Bill.

*I'm convinced that most human misery
is self-inflicted,* says the stoic
who has a job & the full support of his faculty.

They do not torture themselves
because it could have been sunny.
Because I will go back to bed.
Because I will wake up again & again.
Because I will repeat.
I will clean the coffee pot every morning,
dump the cold grounds into my hand,
put my hand under the tap
as if I have unearthed myself.

Obit.

A limit   Cruddy yellow lines on either side   A gap
You won't trespass   Sway your edges
Here   On this platform

Daily   You want nothing more than to
Change   Your   Mind

Let yourself be swayed   One way or the other
Stand on the cautious yellow
Stare down the tunnel & shrug

Who would do this?   Your morbid thought
like a turnstile   Pass through the quotidian thing
This is not news

No Way   To speak it
To delineate   To answer

What else could crush the wind out of you?
Too much is   Hard To Talk About

So let the train enter the station   Let it whirl
up your scarf with such swiftness

You press your palm against it   against your chest

Half sorry

In a familiar place I remember twilight
is divided into three & wish someone
would teach me how to do something
civil with my hands. Last week I
dreamed I lived close to a river
& had a habit to cling to. It would
be helpful to tell someone I am certain
I like rapids better when I can hear
obstructions breaking
the water's surface, but I can't
see them. Days are always getting longer
or shorter & this evening feels
like a sailor's knot, a fixed noose
at the end of a line. I only want
to look at my life through a telescope.
Another lie. I want to stand in a body of water,
cup one hand around the other,
line up my thumbs, & put my lips
to the space & speak. Except
I've never been able to do a loon call
& I am half envious half sorry
when someone does it well enough
for a loon to show up, presumably,
looking for another loon.

Key concept

To grieve is *to adhere to the memory of*
someone or something, as one does to a rule, *closely*,
as an owl's eyes follow a mouse, or *loyally*,
as a wife to a wife, or *unwaveringly*,
as lake to shore, sort of; or, *to divide*,
as an election might do, *as if by a cutting blow*,
like have you seen the news? or, *to split along the grain*
the part of you that remembers
from the part of you that forgets.

Unresolved referent

The ambiguity of *lost* is fixed,
referring to both what can & can't be

recovered. Lately, I self-monitor, losing nothing
that can be recorded. Finding I am whole

days asking: how did a bad thing happen?
Note how I've learned to talk around it.

So when days go by where I couldn't say
what went on, what I had done – well

Yesterday, on the floor, chest down
for who knows how long

I stretched under the bed & found gold hoops – missing
for who knows how long.

They were linked through each other
for who knows how long

like a Venn diagram revealing an overlap
between wanting to live & wanting to die.

Who knows how long
I shook the dust off my sweater

Bad luck elegy

Surely it's bad luck to mourn someone who isn't dead.
It's bad luck to mourn someone who isn't dead

hoping it kills him.
Bad luck to mourn someone you do not miss –

I mean, what happens when a bad thing dies?
This might be accompanied by an elegy, too.

I have never not once seen him since
I quit working the cash at that store in that city.

So if he were dead I wouldn't know it.
So everything would look the same

if my rapist were dead. But his death
surprisingly not something I fantasize.

Maybe it's the *my* of it.
He's mine (!) is what keeps this wish quiet.

If all my friends' rapists were dead, then
what? Maybe E wouldn't have to see him

at the park & ghost before he sees her.
Maybe that'd be pretty good. Maybe

if they were all dead we'd take their ashes, cover our feet,
& show everyone & that would be proof & oh

how we would mourn them. Best to get it
out of the way, to smash a mirror

while yelling their names. To feel
the what of it. What is the word

for something that is yours, given
to you without your asking.

Given too gentle a word.
What belongs to you without belonging.

Saw in half

Once used for a magic trick
she folded herself into an ornate prop box
covered in stars (yellow & white) & darkness:
actually a navy blue.
Under the saw she is
one whole night divided in two
wiggling her fingers & toes
for proof: a body can be OK divided, too.
Wiggling her fingers & toes
one whole night divided in two.
Under the saw she is
actually a navy blue
covered in stars (yellow & white) & darkness:
she folded herself into an ornate prop box
once used for a magic trick.

Superstitions

What future of his might have been spoiled
if we traded superstitions.

In the off season, we sat around bonfires
sharing wine coolers & pilsners,

thinking through our politics: *she loves me, she loves me not,*
he loves me, he loves me not.

He had one hand in his pants,
the other holding an empty can into which he spat

because that was the year all the hockey players
got into chewing tobacco,

& their balls. Naked together
several nights a week

the whole team let us know
every width, length, & diameter

while we figured out the changeroom choreography
of putting on one shirt

while taking off another, our own wish
for luck. There were holes

in the changeroom door
& we knew not to say anything

about who loved us,
who loved us not,

how ruin
skated us quiet

& how loved,
the glare of the ice.

Yesterday, in future tense

The curtain will catch in the fan, making a sound, giving me a dream I'm on a motorboat travelling at a speed at which no heart could rest.

I will wake up & remove the curtain without turning off the fan. Its metal guard has gaps so wide my hand can reach its blades easily, but I will not.

I will go back to sleep & wake up & sleep & wake up.

While getting dressed, I will pause so many times I will hear the local news on the radio twice & still I will end up wearing what I wore yesterday.

Searching for an email from my father from last August, I will type my aunt's name.

Thian Hoei

After reading a short story about an unknown woman dying, her unknownness the story's centre, I will write a summary & make the questions about her, which are actually about the narrator, about myself.

Stories about the dead will be about the dead.

I will tell myself & my philodendron I want to leave the house. I won't mean it, but the plant's leaves will be leaning toward the window.

When I'm hungry, I will text Liz to ask her what I should I eat. Then I will write *But also, I want to sleep forever.*

She will write back, *I get that. Get cheezies.*

I will love her for recognizing my hyperbole as not-so-hyper.

She is sad, too, she will tell me she has questions, too. Her questions will be like my questions will be like old questions will be like new like the stories about the dead will be about the dead as much as they will be about the living feeling like dying because we will feel like dying because we feel like dying sometimes.

Obit.

An exit,
though I notice

many of the fire escapes
in Montreal duplexes

are stairs within storage spaces
leading to lower storage spaces

& I fantasize about riding the metro
all day, as if

its motion might
move me.

Obit.

I bet everything old will be new again. A commute.
Everything
hot will get cold again. Rush hour will summon those who can

take it, clothed in mostly black & grey. I will risk telling
everyone something
with my posture. This is not a daily funeral,

it's just what it looks like. I bet the rush
will slow down again
& one winter morning I will find myself dying,

wrapped in too many layers of wool. A person wearing
pink lipstick
will close their eyes & the crowd will feel gentle.

My psyche is welded into the wrong shape.
Unsturdy. Unlike
the pole I rest my hand on, my head on my hand.

So what, I like to look at my reflection. I bet every distraction
is a main event.
Someone with grey hair & forest-green corduroy pants

will wave off someone asking for change.
That is an event.
I bet every hand has performed that action. I bet he reads

the obits., like I scroll through the timeline, & I bet
I'm taking a risk
when I don't know the dead.

Notes

p. 7: The epigraph from Claudia Rankine comes from *Don't Let Me Be Lonely: An American Lyric* (Graywolf Press, 2004).

p. 7: The epigraph from Yiyun Li comes from *Dear Friend, from My Life I Write to You in Your Life* (Random House, 2017).

p. 11: The quote from Wendy Xu is from a poem called 'The News' (found on PoetryFoundation.org © 2015, Wendy Xu).

p. 12: The unnamed journalist quoted in 'Dead theories' is Glenn Greenwald (on Democracy Now!, May 25, 2017).

pp. 12–13: The words from Ruth Stone are from a poem called 'Advice' (*No more masks!: An anthology of poems by women*, Anchor Press, 1973).

p. 14: The phrase '(impossible) to theorize the real' is from a poem in *Furious* by Erin Mouré (House of Anansi, 1988).

p. 16: The words from Hannah Gamble are from a poem called 'Most People Would Rather Not' (*Poetry Magazine*, October, 2013).

p. 18: In 'When,' all the text set in italics is from Jill Stauffer's *Ethical Loneliness: The Injustic of Not Being Heard* (Columbia University Press, 2015), except for 'the disturbance of self-regard is absent in mourning,' which is from Sigmund Freud's 'Mourning and Melancholia.' The italics in 'The jilt' are from the same text.

p. 22–23: The italics in 'Call it' are from Judith Butler's *Precarious Life: The Powers of Mourning and Violence* (Verso, 2006), and the title of a Juliana Spahr poem (*This Connection of Everyone with Lungs*, University of California Press, 2005).

p. 24: 'Aesthetic distance' uses text from Robert Archambeau's essay 'Aesthetic Interference,' published in Hyperallergic (December 24, 2016).

p. 29: I first learned about the story of Euripides from Anne Carson's *Nox* (New Directions, 2010).

p. 37: The words from Theresa Hak Kyung Cha are from *Dictee* (2nd ed., University of California, 2009, originally published 1982).

p. 41: The words from Li-Young Lee are from a poem called 'The Cleaving' (*The City in Which I Love You*, BOA Editions, 1990).

p. 66: 'Brothers' is a short story by Sherwood Anderson (from *100 Years of the Best American Short Stories*, Houghton Mifflin Harcourt, 2015).

pp. 67–68: The text in square brackets in 'Mother, wife, sister' is by Shoshana Felman (*What Does a Woman Want?: Reading and Sexual Difference*, Johns Hopkins University Press, 1993).

p. 71–72: The quotes from Rebecca Solnit are from her essay 'Men Explain *Lolita* to Me,' published on LitHub (December 17, 2015).

p. 73–76: The Baudelaire poems are based on my limited knowledge of French, translations done by William Aggeler, and a deep discomfort with the originals.

p. 82: I wrote 'I can't say I wanted that' after a conversation with Marcela Huerta (author of *Tropico*, Metatron Press, 2017).

p. 85: The words from C. D. Wright are from a poem called 'Our Dust' (*Like Something Flying Backwards*, Bloodaxe Books, 2007).

Acknowledgments

Thank you to the editors who published previous versions of some of these poems in *The Puritan, Vallum, carte blanche, PRISM, The Walrus, Room Magazine,* & *Best Canadian Poetry 2018*; & thanks to Anstruther Press for the chapbook.

I am grateful to everyone at Coach House for guiding me through the process of bookmaking, especially Susan Holbrook for keeping me thinking through every bit and piece of every poem.

Thank you to Mary di Michele & Stephanie Bolster for your attention & encouragement; & thanks to workshop peers for all kinds of critiques. Thank you to Karen Solie, & Colettte Bryce for talking me through rewriting this collection. Thank you to Ocean Vuong for generous reading & conversation, for making me feel seen. Thank you to Sina Queyras for mentorship, for opportunities to speak & be heard, for reminding me to write every day.

In admiration, I am thankful to Phoebe Wang for holding the door open & inviting me in. Thank you to Natalie Eilbert for taking time to read & respond to these poems, & for writing a book I needed to read.

For friendship, first first reads, & kind words, thank you, Karissa LaRocque, & Eli Tareq. Thanks, Lauren Turner, for coffee dates throughout writing all this, & for text check-ins on rough days <3

Many of these poems are for Liz Went – I'm living for your friendship. Many of these poems are for those who feel fractioned, who call themselves half, or mixed. Many poems are for those who have mostly tough days, bed days, dark days, not-OK days. I see you. If you've made it this far, holding this thing in your hands, thank you.

Most of all, I am grateful to my partner, Surah Field-Green, for living with me while I wrote these poems, for keeping me alive, for love.

Tess Liem is a queer writer living in Montreal, Tiotia:ke, the traditional territory of the Kanien'kehá:ka. She is the author of the chapbook *Tell everybody I say hi* (Anstruther, 2017) and her writing has appeared in *Plenitude, Room Magazine, PRISM, Best Canadian Poetry 2018,* and elsewhere. Her essay 'Rice Cracker' won the Constance Rooke Creative Nonfiction Prize in 2015.

Typeset in Arno and Gibson

Printed at the Coach House on bpNichol Lane in Toronto, Ontario, on Zephyr Antique Laid paper, which was manufactured, acid-free, in Saint-Jérôme, Quebec, from second-growth forests. This book was printed with vegetable-based ink on a 1973 Heidelberg kord offset litho press. Its pages were folded on a Baumfolder, gathered by hand, bound on a Sulby Auto-Minabinda, and trimmed on a Polar single-knife cutter.

Edited by Susan Holbrook
Designed by Crystal Sikma
Cover by Crystal Sikma
Author photo by Surah Field-Green

Coach House Books
80 bpNichol Lane
Toronto ON M5S 3J4
Canada

416 979 2217
800 367 6360

mail@chbooks.com
www.chbooks.com